D1716236

Zoom In on
In the Sky

Moon

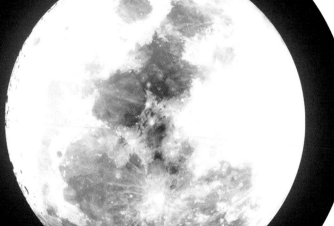

Andrea Rivera

abdopublishing.com

Published by Abdo Zoom™, PO Box 398166, Minneapolis, Minnesota 55439. Copyright © 2017 by Abdo Consulting Group, Inc. International copyrights reserved in all countries. No part of this book may be reproduced in any form without written permission from the publisher. Abdo Zoom™ is a trademark and logo of Abdo Consulting Group, Inc.

Printed in the United States of America, North Mankato, Minnesota
102016
012017

THIS BOOK CONTAINS
RECYCLED MATERIALS

Cover Photo: Shukaylova Zinaida/Shutterstock Images
Interior Photos: Shukaylova Zinaida/Shutterstock Images, 1; iStockphoto, 4–5, 6; NASA's Scientific Visualization Studio, 5, 16–17; NASA's Goddard Space Flight Center, 7; Shutterstock Images, 8, 9, 19, 21; Edwin E. Aldrin Jr./NASA, 10–11; Neil A. Armstrong/NASA, 11; NASA, 12, 13, 14–15, 18; Craig Rubadoux/ Florida Today/AP Images, 15;

Editor: Emily Temple
Series Designer: Madeline Berger
Art Direction: Dorothy Toth

Publisher's Cataloging-in-Publication Data
Names: Rivera, Andrea, author.
Title: Moon / by Andrea Rivera.
Description: Minneapolis, MN : Abdo Zoom, 2017. | Series: In the sky |
    Includes bibliographical references and index.
Identifiers: LCCN 2016948919 | ISBN 9781680799323 |
    ISBN 9781624025181 (ebook) | ISBN 9781624025747 (Read-to-me ebook)
Subjects: LCSH: Moon--Juvenile literature.
Classification: DDC 523.3--dc23
LC record available at http://lccn.loc.gov/2016948919

Table of Contents

4

Moons are round objects.

Science

They orbit larger planets. Moons can be different shapes, sizes, and colors.

Earth has one moon. It is about 4.5 billion years old. Scientists believe a space object hit Earth. Pieces broke off.

The pieces connected years later.
They formed the Moon.

Technology

People first observed the moon in the early 1600s. They used **telescopes**.

They drew maps of what they saw. New telescopes show the Moon more clearly.

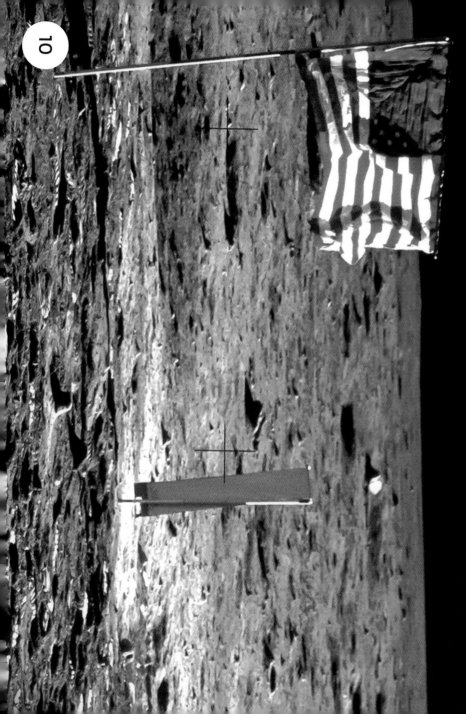

Engineering

Humans first landed on the Moon in 1969.

The astronauts wore spacesuits.

The suits had many layers. Nothing could get inside.

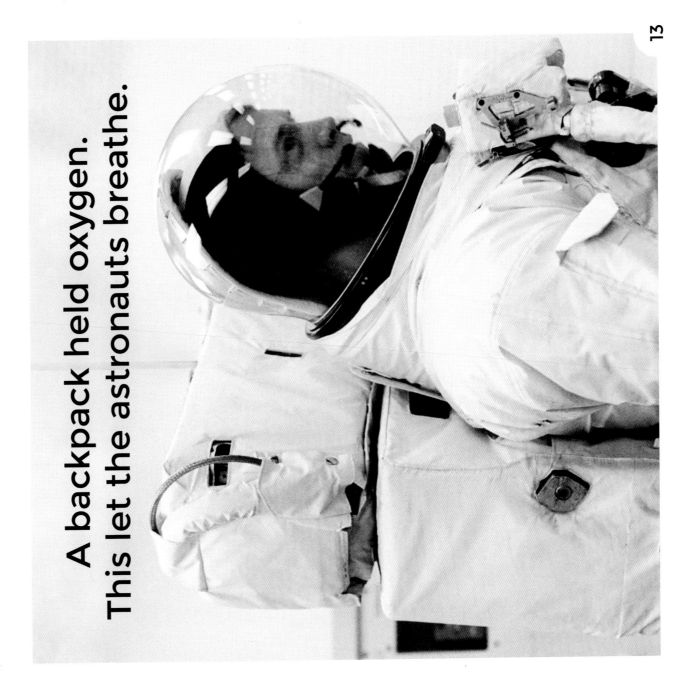

A backpack held oxygen. This let the astronauts breathe.

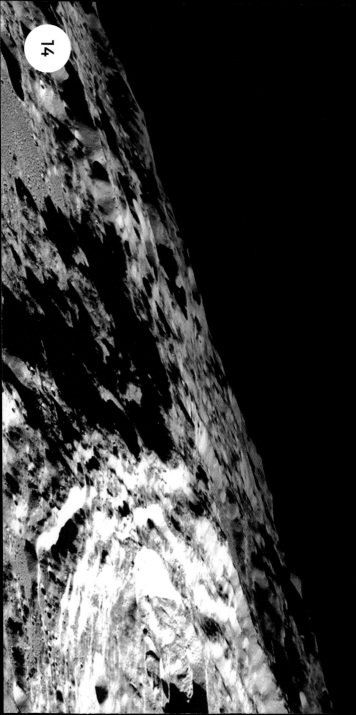

The Moon is covered in large **craters**. These spots can make the Moon look like a face.

Art

This has inspired many artists.

The Moon orbits Earth each month.

Math

It goes through eight phases.
Its shadow changes each time.

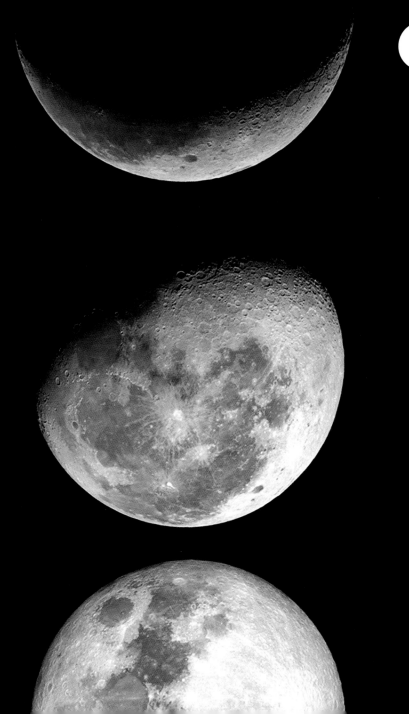

A full moon looks like a circle.

A crescent moon looks like the letter C.

Key Stats

- Earth is about four times bigger than the Moon.

- The Moon is around 250,000 miles (400,000 km) away from Earth.

- The Moon is the second brightest object in the sky. The sun is the brightest.

- The Moon does not create light. It reflects light from the sun.

Glossary

astronaut – someone who travels to space.

crater – a dip in the ground shaped like a large bowl.

orbit – to travel around something, usually in an oval path.

phase – a regularly occurring stage of change.

telescope – an instrument that uses lenses, mirrors, or both to make faraway objects look closer.

Booklinks

For more information
on the Moon, please visit
booklinks.abdopublishing.com

Zoom In on STEAM!

Learn even more with the Abdo Zoom
STEAM database. Check out
abdozoom.com for more information.

Index